What's happening?
At the zoo

Heather Amery
Illustrated by Stephen Cartwright

Consultant: Betty Root

Looking at the animals

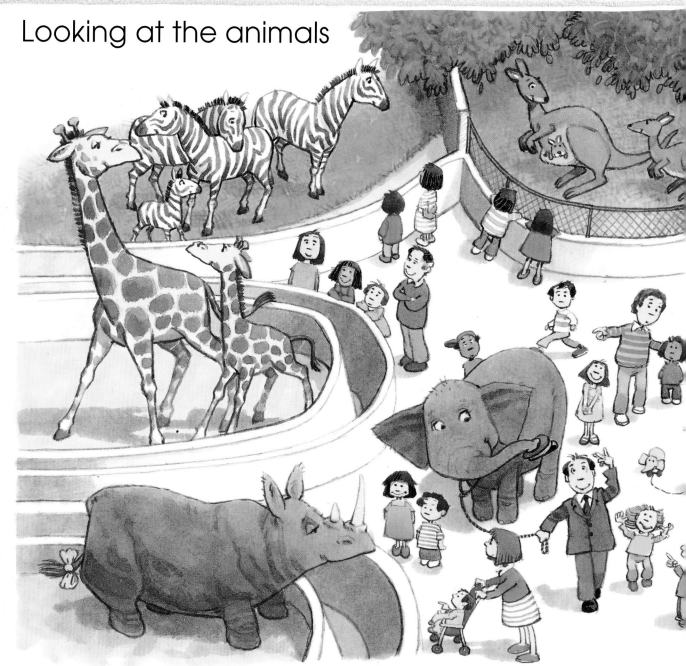

Can you find the zoo keeper?
What are they doing?

How many different animals can you see?
Which ones have babies?

Watching the lions

How many lion cubs are there?
Which one is going to get into trouble?

Can you find a white mouse?
What's stuck in the tree?

Looking at the birds

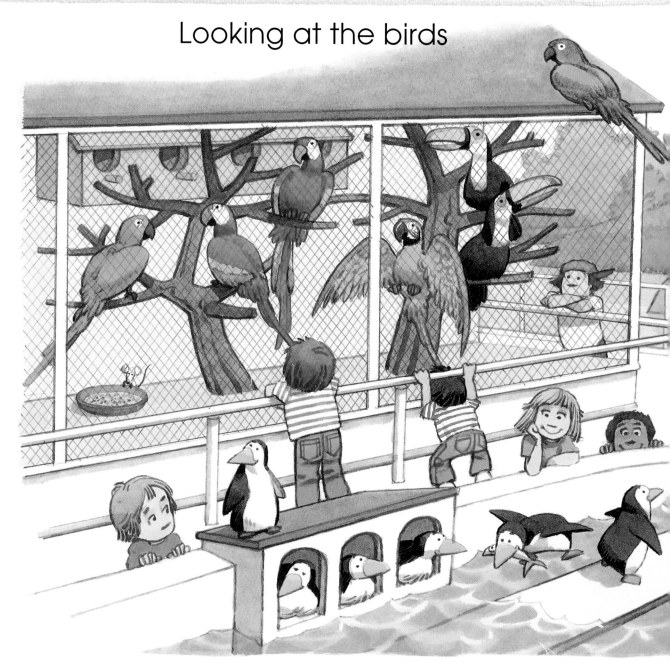

How many different kinds of birds can you see?
Which ones have the biggest beaks?

What do penguins like to eat?
How many birds are swimming?

In the aquarium

Which fish have stripes?
Can you find all the yellow fish?

Do you know the names of all these creatures?
How many people are looking at them?

Bathtime for a polar bear

How many cubs are there?
How many children are wearing hats?

Playtime for the dolphins

How many dolphins are there?
Which ones have red rings?

The chimpanzees and the gorillas

Chimpanzees have pale faces and gorillas have black faces.
What are all the chimpanzees doing?

How many baby gorillas can you see?
Which fruits do chimpanzees and gorillas like to eat?

In the children's zoo

How many rabbits can you count?
What other animals can you see?

What are all the goats doing?
Who has lost a shoe?

Animal puzzle

Match the animals' heads with their legs.

First Published in 1984, Usborne Publishing Ltd, Usborne House, 83-85 Saffron Hill, London EC1N 8RT.
© 1992, 1984, Usborne Publising Ltd.

First published in America March 1993
Universal Edition